T0146872

Everyday Wellbeing for Mums

Thirty Life-Changing Tools to Help You Feel Successful as You Raise Your Children

RHIANNON COLAROSSI

BALBOA.PRESS
A DIVISION OF HAY HOUSE

Balboa Press books may be ordered through booksellers or by contacting:

Balboa Press
A Division of Hay House
1663 Liberty Drive
Bloomington, IN 47403
www.balboapress.com.au
1 (877) 407-4847

Print information available on the last page.

ISBN: 978-1-5043-2072-6 (sc)
ISBN: 978-1-5043-2073-3 (e)

Balboa Press rev. date: 03/11/2020

Contents

Dedication

To you, for doing the work every day to raise
your children and for caring enough about your
wellbeing to read this book. This is for you.

Thank you for picking up this book. I know your time is
precious, so I'll get straight to the point. If your children
are between 0 and twelve, and you want to feel your
absolute best as you raise them, then this book is a must-
read for you.

I hope it will be your go-to wellbeing guide, your
toolkit in times when you are stressed, exhausted, and
overwhelmed. It contains thirty highly practical and
effective wellbeing tools that you can easily incorporate
into your day, when you have little time to take care of
yourself.

Integrating wellbeing tools into your daily routine can
make a huge difference in how you feel. Taking time
to slow down; appreciating the good; letting things go;

saying no more often; and enjoying an entire cup of hot tea in one sitting are all examples of simple tweaks that can help you enjoy a happy and well-balanced life.

Over the past thirty-five years, I've spent lots of time in the education system, as a student, a teacher, a school wellbeing leader, and a parent of two gorgeous children, Jonathan and Madeleine. My passion for seeing children flourish in this world is stronger than ever; I firmly believe that you hold the key to helping your child thrive.

Back in 2002, during my very first year as a teacher, I learnt something they don't tell you at university: that a mum's wellbeing impacts a child's happiness and learning ability in the classroom.

As a young teacher, I observed the constant busyness and non-presence of some parents. I didn't just notice this pattern in times of struggle such as a divorce, moving house, or death in the family. It was just as apparent with the everyday autopilot way of being. I admittedly didn't understand it at the time and often judged the situation, as I wasn't yet a mum myself. However, I knew with crystal-clear certainty that if mums knew the value of their wellbeing, like I did, they would choose to slow down and be more present. They would take a moment to look at their child's drawing on the wall, to kiss them goodbye using eye contact, to make rushing less of a habit, and to do all of this from a place of loving and calm.

It's become my mission, as a mum, to share this life-changing knowledge with those who are willing to read my book. I know for a fact that when you look after your own wellbeing, not only do you thrive, but your child does too. This is the true essence of family wellbeing and a priceless gift to share with your child.

Despite the chaos and challenges that are often part of daily life, you deserve to feel at peace, every single day. And it's possible to live a happy and peace-filled life while raising young children. I know this because it's the life I'm living. That's not to say I don't feel challenged constantly with the demands of each child: ensuring they arrive at school on time, with everything they need; leaving the house without losing my marbles (yes, I still have to repeatedly ask my children to put on their shoes); cleaning up after breakfast; navigating their meltdowns; organising dinner; and the list goes on. However, there is an underlying feeling within that all is okay, and this calm presence helps me feel supported, even when everything around me feels like it's falling apart. The best news is that you can have this feeling too. With a little focus and commitment, you can feel good each day. I know if I can do it, you can absolutely do it too. I'm just like you: a mum trying to do my best and be my best, not only for myself but for my family.

I've practised these tools consistently over the past ten years, and I'm so excited to share my journey with you. I hope that after reading this book, you'll incorporate some of these wellbeing tools into your own life. And remember, *practising* the tools is where you'll find the wellbeing gold. The ripple effect that ensues not only transforms your day (and life) but also positively impacts all those you care about. This book is for you, and I'm honoured to be a part of your wellbeing journey.

How to Use the Tools to Elevate Your Everyday Wellbeing

I've outlined some ideas about how you might like to use my tools in your daily routine to make sure you get the most out of this book, without feeling overwhelmed.

A brilliant way to begin is with the Getting Clear tool. Clarity is a wellbeing superpower. Knowing how you're doing in the five wellbeing dimensions provides you with a strong foundation to create your wellbeing goals. After reading about this tool, you'll be drawn to the back of the book, where you'll find the Wellbeing Reflection Activity. This clarifying exercise is the perfect starting point for your wellbeing journey.

Once you complete the Wellbeing Reflection Activity, you may decide to try one wellbeing tool for a week. My suggestion for this is Wellbeing Tool 2: the Positive Action Plan (PAP). It's hands-down my favourite wellbeing tool. Using this super simple, highly effective wellbeing tool each day for seven days will help you start feeling in control of your wellbeing.

Another way to approach the book is to scan through the tools and try a tool that jumps out at you. There's no right way; however, going slow and implementing one tool at a time will ensure you don't feel overwhelmed. By taking your time and focusing on one tool, you'll notice measurable results such as the feeling of wellbeing success, which means feeling like yourself, like everything is okay, and feeling that you can handle any major meltdowns, household disasters, or back-chat challenges that come your way.

This book will support you in building up your wellbeing toolkit, one tool (or wellbeing tweak) at a time. I hope you feel the positive energy that emanates from the pages in this book because I wrote it for *you*, so let's get started.

Note: If you are really struggling, please seek help. At the back of this book, there is a list of some places where readers in Australia can find support.

1

The Wellbeing Priority Tool

Beautiful mum, wellbeing is a choice, and you make the decision to prioritise it by affirming to yourself, *I choose wellbeing.* You may have hit rock bottom, be experiencing sheer exhaustion, or simply feel flat and wish to feel uplifted. Wherever you are right now is the perfect starting point. So hold onto your hat because from this day onwards, your decision to make your wellbeing (and therefore your happiness) a priority will open the door to a life of feeling good, and that's exciting.

Take a moment now to say out loud, "Yes, yes, yes," because this is the true starting point of your wellbeing journey. One year from now, you'll celebrate your first Wellversary! Your Wellversary is your wellbeing anniversary, the day your declaration to the universe was heard. Make today the first day of your journey back to your true self.

I celebrate my Wellversary on 17 February, and as I write this, I've just celebrated my tenth one, a decade of wellbeing.

Wellbeing is a daily priority, and I know that without it, I'd be anxious, stressed out, unhappy, judgemental, and high-strung. My husband will tell you that I still operate in these modes occasionally (thanks, hubby, for keeping me off my wellbeing high horse), but the point is, they don't dominate my daily life.

The catalyst for my wellbeing journey came after my son, Jonathan, arrived almost seven weeks early; I had pre-eclampsia, a diaphragmatic hernia, and a partially collapsed lung that was causing immense pain. Consequently, I was induced early because both my baby and I were at risk.

On our second wedding anniversary, when Jonathan was two months old, I was scheduled to have my diaphragmatic hernia repaired.

After the hernia operation, I began to go downhill quickly and was struggling to breathe. I just couldn't seem to suck enough oxygen in, even with the giant oxygen mask. I was literally gasping for every breath.

Breathing had been something I'd always taken for granted, but now it was my number one priority; I was well and truly in survival mode. The doctors decided I must go back into the operating theatre so they could reinflate my lung. Waiting for them to prepare themselves (and me) for the operation felt like an eternity.

I've never felt so helpless, I've never felt so scared, and I've never wanted to live more than I did in that moment. As they wheeled me towards the theatre's double doors, fear consumed me; I wasn't ready to die. I was twenty-eight years old and was meant to be starting my life as a mum. This wasn't how it was supposed to be.

I woke up some hours later, breathing through a tube; I remember feeling a huge sense of relief. I had made it. I had just been given a second chance. As I rested in the recovery room with the breathing tube still in place, I had time to deeply reflect on my life.

During that time, I asked myself these three life-changing questions:

- What have I been doing with my life?
- Am I happy?
- What will I do differently now?

Over the next few hours, I had many realisations.

I realised I had been moving through life on autopilot. I was just going through the motions: school, university, work, marriage, and kids. Even though many of those experiences had brought me joy, I didn't feel happy or at peace with myself.

The biggest realisation came when I learnt that I'd been living my life from a place of fear. I feared being judged, pushing the status quo, stepping into the arena, not being enough, being a failure, and most of all, I feared living a happy and successful life on my terms.

I knew if I was going to live my best life, I needed to start taking the reins. At that moment, I began appreciating and loving myself. I would no longer seek approval or permission from anyone else. I finally felt empowered to create the life I desired.

Throughout this book, you'll come to know your worth and learn that you are enough, exactly as you are. You'll soon come to realise that you deserve the best and can show up each day as a happy and calm mum.

Inspired Action: Mark down today's date in your diary.

Today is a celebration. Why? Because by marking this date down in your diary, you've automatically created your Wellversary date, which definitely calls for a celebration. You have made your wellbeing a priority; you're officially on your priority list. One year from now, your Wellversary, you'll look back and see how far you have come and how much you have grown. Your wellbeing will have improved by leaps and bounds, and you'll be filled with appreciation and joy for deciding to make yourself a priority.

2

The Positive Action Plan Tool

Completing the Positive Action Plan is my favourite way to begin the day. All too often, we wake up in the morning and dive immediately into a negative rant such as, "I can't be bothered getting up. I need more sleep. I don't feel like making the lunches or going to work." It's for this reason I decided to develop the Positive Action Plan.

The PAP tool helps guide you to positively set the tone for your day, right from the moment you wake up, before any negativity has a chance to take hold.

The way your day begins tends to be the way your day continues to flow, and the morning rush can be a chaotic time. Being conscious of your wellbeing from the moment you open your eyes makes a huge difference in how your day unfolds.

The transformational power of the PAP tool is undeniable. It's about taking responsibility for your life every morning.

When my two children were young, they woke up four to five times every single night for the first three years of their little lives; this meant six years of severe sleep deprivation. I was recovering from my operation, moving house, undergoing a home renovation, and experiencing financial strain.

It was a crazy time in our lives. I was exhausted and didn't want to get out of bed and face the day ahead; however, the PAP tool made sure I did. It kept me present with my young children and kept my marriage on track when it very easily could have fallen apart. The PAP tool saved me from a stressed-out life, and it can save you too.

Inspired Action, Part One: Creating your PAP.

From the moment you wake up each morning, ask yourself these three questions:

1. How do I want to feel today?
2. What can I appreciate right now?
3. What are my top three priorities for the day?

In other words, create your day. Begin by setting your intention, add a pinch of appreciation, and finish off with three specific actions for the day.

You may also like to invite your children to set their intentions for the day. I often do this with them in the car on the way to school. This is one way to share your wellbeing practice without it feeling too heavy or another boring Mum topic that will cause them to tune out.

This simple and practical wellbeing tool can help you (and your children) feel calm during this demanding time and ready for the day ahead.

Inspired Action, Part Two: The PAP check-in.

One of the benefits of doing a morning PAP is that it doubles as a daily self-check-in tool. To check-in with yourself at any point during the day, simply ask yourself, "How am I feeling? Am I in alignment with the intention I set during my morning PAP?" By bringing your focus to your feelings, you become mindful about how you actually feel.

Once you're aware of how you feel you have the choice to respond in a way that nurtures your wellbeing. For example, if you feel stress creeping in (and you're far from the intention you set yourself), you may decide to pause and take a few conscious breaths. Being mindful of your feelings is empowering and helps guide you back to your desired intention. Every choice you make throughout the day, big or small, naturally impacts how you feel in any given moment.

Inspired Action, Part Three: The PAP celebration.

A morning PAP also has significant benefits as the day comes to an end. Each night (around the dinner table as a family, or as you lay down to go to sleep), spend a minute celebrating what you most enjoyed about your day. How was it successful? Mums are often experts at recounting the mistakes we made or recalling the list of things we didn't get done. However, by setting those top three priorities in your PAP each morning, you (and your family) can look back and celebrate the little things you achieved, ensuring you start and end the day on a positive note.

3

The Getting Clear Tool

Awareness and reflection are essential for living each day as your best self. This tool encourages you to take a look at your life and assess how you're really going. When you do so, you'll be sure to have no regrets.

Every day, through the choices you make, you steer your life in one direction or another, either towards living in alignment with your best life or in the opposite direction. By pausing and focusing on how things are going, you have the opportunity to decide if you're happy with how your life is travelling or if it's not in alignment with your core values. Taking an honest look helps you know that the only person standing in your way is you. You have the power to change your choices.

We all desire to be happy, but it's up to you to take charge of your life. By this, I don't mean you need to control every aspect of it but rather integrate small positive actions into your daily routine; this sets the tone for how you're going to live each and every day.

Eleven years prior to writing this book, I had a huge light-bulb moment. I realised I was giving my husband my leftovers. I'd been with Nick for eight years, and within half an hour of completing my Wellbeing Reflection Activity, which you'll find at the back of this book, I had to face the truth: I was taking our relationship for granted. I'd been too busy pleasing everyone else around me. And when it came to him, I had nothing left to give. I hadn't prioritised our relationship, I wasn't being present with him, and I wasn't appreciating him. I couldn't believe it. It was ridiculous. He was the man I chose to spend my life with, but the reality was, I was treating him more as a dumping ground after a frustrating day. It was hard to take responsibility for this, but I knew I had the power to change it. From that moment on, I decided to appreciate him more, to be more conscious of how I felt, and to not take my negative feelings out on him. It was the beginning of an emotionally mature relationship.

Inspired Action: Be courageous and explore how you are really going in all five wellbeing dimensions: physical, social, mental, spiritual, and emotional. In order to take positive action, notice which dimensions you're thriving in and which ones need more of your time, love, and energy. To reflect on your wellbeing, go to the back of your book, where you'll find the Wellbeing Reflection Activity. The first time you do this, it may feel a little overwhelming, but the clarity and wellbeing that arise are well worth the effort.

I'm truly grateful that I took the time to stop and check in. I had a feeling that something was out of alignment, but I didn't know what. At age twenty-eight, I finally had clarity on where I was at and what action I needed to take.

The clarity you receive by delving deeper and reflecting on your wellbeing will enlighten you. This awareness is the perfect starting point to affirm all the good in your life and helps you to set goals and actions to strengthen the dimensions that you've neglected.

4

The All About Action Tool

Let's dive into some more inspired action, lovely. Sometimes, simply starting is the best way to move forward. The perfect time is now.

Using your newly found clarity from the wellbeing reflection activity, set yourself a goal, followed by some mini actions to help you achieve that objective. Starting with a small, achievable goal is a practical way to kick-start your wellbeing momentum in a gentle yet powerful way.

When my kids were young, my goal was really simple: Be present with them. It was all I needed to keep myself on track. It helped me feel like I was doing a decent job as a mum (mainly because I wasn't yelling at them all the time). At this stage of my motherhood journey, being

13

present with them meant I sometimes left the washing on the line for weeks because I didn't have the energy to bring it in, and I'd only do the dishes when I needed them. When well-meaning family and friends would come to visit and notice the state of the house or the pile of dishes, I'd simply say to them, "I know, but they weren't my priority today." I was struggling with sleep deprivation, yet I wanted to feel like I was doing a good job. I knew that if I tried to keep my home sparkling clean as well as a trying to be a calm mum, it would have broken me. I had to focus on what was most important to me: my children, my husband, and my wellbeing.

If I'd tried to be a Supermum, I'd have yelled a lot, been stressed out, resented my husband, and felt hard done by. I wanted better. My children deserved the best of me, and it was up to me to take charge, even on minimal sleep. So I practised being present every single day. This one simple goal saved my sanity, helped me to enjoy the mess and chaos of motherhood, and saved my marriage.

Inspired Action: Take out your diary, turn on your laptop, or flip to a new page in your wellbeing notebook, because today, you'll set yourself one wellbeing goal, along with one or two mini actions that will propel you towards achieving this goal. Start by writing the following heading: "My Wellbeing Goal for the Week."

Beneath your goal, write one or two actions that you can commit to doing each day for seven days.

Each day for the following week, read over your wellbeing goal and carry out your mini actions. I've given some examples of goals and mini actions below.

Wellbeing Goal and Mini Action Examples

Example 1

Goal: To feel calmer in my role as mum.

Mini action 1: Each morning as I wake, I'll say to myself, "I'm doing the best I can to raise my children. I'm a good mum, and today is going to be a calm day."

Mini action 2: I'll take a deep breath before responding to my children today.

Example 2

Goal: To feel more successful as I raise my children.

Mini action 1: I'll pause throughout the day to reflect and celebrate all that I do in my role as a mum. I know that these mini pauses will help me to slow down and nurture my everyday wellbeing.

Mini action 2: I'll compliment myself when I notice my actions and words are coming from kind intentions. (You're a successful mum, and being kind to yourself is wellbeing success.)

Example 3

Goal: To feel good about my body.

Mini action 1: As I wake up each morning, I will stretch for five minutes while reflecting on my body love mantra. Today's mantra: "I love my body, as it helps me to do so much for others and myself. I make nourishing choices and treat my body with respect and kindness."

Mini action 2: I wear the clothes I feel the most wonderful wearing. Remember that it's not what you wear; it's how you feel in what you wear that really matters.

Example 4

Goal: To be present with my loved ones.

Mini action 1: I'll put my phone away when I'm having a conversation with anyone in my home.

Mini action 2: I'll listen with the intention of understanding and being fully present with them, not to give advice, blame, criticise, dismiss, or judge.

5

The Go Slow Today Tool

In today's busy world, the power of going slow is greatly underestimated but is more important than ever. With anxiety and mental health issues on the rise (for mums as well as the younger generation), it's time to slow down.

In fact, going slow is one of my favourite wellbeing tools. It's also the perfect tool to share with your children. Can you imagine how wonderful it would feel if you and all those in your life decided that going slow was the way to be? I'd like to think that one day, slow will be the new black.

It's no secret that many of us feel that if we rush around as quickly as possible, we'll achieve more, get more done, and feel more successful. However, the opposite is almost always the case.

When you rush, you often make mistakes (which require more time to fix), you say things you wish you hadn't (usually to our partners and children), and you feel frazzled as a result. This way of living is not a sign of success and definitely not a sign that you're living in wellbeing alignment.

Inspired Action, Part One: Decide that slow will be your new black. Take three deep breaths a few times throughout your day, which will help you approach your tasks with calm energy. You may tend to hold your breath or breathe shallowly throughout the day, but by consciously taking deep breaths, you suppress cortisol (a stress hormone), and this simple action acts as an on-the-go wellbeing reset. In fact, while you're reading about it, take a moment now to enjoy three deep breaths. The beauty of taking three deep breaths is that you can do it anytime you catch yourself rushing. You have the ability to pause at any time, take three deep breaths, and continue going about your day in slow mode.

The morning rush is one key situation where taking three deep breaths and going slowly is important. It's the perfect opportunity to practice this tool. This precious time sets the tone for the day and often dictates how events will flow. By choosing to go slowly in the morning, you'll give yourself the opportunity to release any anxiety that rushing would usually cause, and you'll continue the day feeling calm.

When I was still finding my wellbeing feet, I began to notice the difference my morning routine (prior to the kids waking up) impacted how the rest of the morning flowed. A clear pattern soon emerged. On the mornings when I didn't set myself up for success (doing my Positive Action Plan and meditating), I (and everyone else in the house) fell apart. We would often end up rushing out the door, feeling upset or stressed. After dropping the kids off, I'd feel awful; I'd dwell on it, and guilt would start to set in. I knew it was up to me to set the tone each morning; sending the children to school with that negative energy was no longer okay. This was the catalyst for making my wellbeing morning routine non-negotiable.

Consciously creating your mornings is empowering and ensures that you're far better equipped to manage the countless requests, complaints, arguments, lost shoes, and refusals to get dressed. It can literally be life-changing for you and your children.

Inspired Action, Part Two: Decide to create a morning wellbeing routine that sets your day up for success. Commit to doing this consistently for at least ten days, and notice how this shifts your energy and the positive impact it has in your home. Noticing the results will help you to make your morning routine a non-negotiable practice, one that everyone will benefit from, especially during the morning rush.

Choose to begin your day with a wellbeing routine and move through your day in slow mode. Be aware of how this feels, knowing that you created it. You'll feel centred and present, and it won't be too long until it becomes your normal way of being.

While many of the tools in this book are perfect to share with your family, you may find the Go Slow Today tool to be one of the best. My family personally love this one, and when we're feeling rushed, we gently remind each other that it's okay to take our time and slow down. Teaching children the go-slow tool helps them to manage feelings of anxiety when they're under pressure, while still being in a safe environment. All you need to do is simply lead the way.

6

The No Tech and Connect Tool

The power of in-person, presence-filled connection is sacred.

Meaningful connection is something that we all crave. In fact, a recent happiness study (spanning seventy-five years) conducted by Harvard University found that meaningful social connection is necessary for sustained happiness.

We live in a world where our phones are like an extension of ourselves, and most of society has succumbed to the head down (in the phone) disease. We must start to prioritise our everyday connections. The little ways you do this matter, such as looking up, putting your phone away, and truly getting back to the basics of connecting with others. Quality relationships protect your mind, body, and happiness over the long term.

Inspired Action: Make time to connect (free of technology or expectations) with a loved one today. Schedule in as little as ten minutes together to sit and chat; to cuddle; to eat or walk together; or to simply be in the moment (leave the phone in the car, or just turn it off).

I understand that sometimes, you need your phone; however, you can't put a price on uninterrupted connection with your child or others you care about. This precious connection time reassures them that they are enough (without actually saying it) and, more importantly, communicates that they matter to you. It helps create a long-lasting bond that you are setting in motion right now.

In our home, we have a "people first" rule. This means that whenever someone enters the room for the first time, no matter what we're doing, we stop and say hello. If my children are watching a show and someone comes to visit, they pause the show and acknowledge them. When we want to send a text, we do so after we finish chatting with the person in front of us, not during. I remember watching a TED Talk that said even holding your phone when talking to someone, or putting it on the table where you can see it, sends them the message that the phone is your priority.

We're social beings by nature, and cultivating deep connections in our relationships helps to boost our social wellbeing. Carving out time in your demanding day to connect and to be totally present with a loved one will do absolute wonders for your wellbeing, while also deepening your bond with them. This is wellbeing in action; what a priceless way to spend your time.

7

The Self-Kindness Tool

Oh, this is a biggie. As a mum, you're prone to being hard on yourself. You feel like you're not good enough, not doing enough, not being enough, not succeeding enough, not happy enough, not calm enough, not fit enough, and the list goes on.

So why are you so hard on yourself? Surely your default isn't to criticise yourself or to punish yourself if you drop the ball for a minute or two. Without delving too deeply, this is the brain trying to protect you so that you stay safe in fight-or-flight mode. Unfortunately, however, it creates an unhappy storm within, which negatively impacts your wellbeing.

During my teens and early twenties, I was constantly in a negative conversation with myself but was completely unaware of it. It was just the norm for me; being kind to myself wasn't even on my radar. When I wasn't beating myself up with my own thoughts, I was replaying conversations and working out what I'd say next time. I was in a constant state of negativity. I wasn't responding to the world around me; I was reacting.

Self-kindness is an essential wellbeing tool for mums, and it took me twenty-eight years to work it out. I don't want you to waste any time. Self-kindness permission has been granted.

In 2009, my wake-up call helped me realise how pointless my self-criticism was and how it had been depleting my wellbeing. I didn't want to bring this negative habit into my motherhood journey, as I knew the harder I was on myself, the harder I was on all those around me. You don't have to wait for a wake-up call; you can decide to be kind to yourself right now. And get ready because this wellbeing tweak alone will bring so many positive experiences into your life.

Inspired Action: Ask yourself, "How can I be kinder to myself right now?" When you're criticising yourself for something you said or did, or something you didn't say or do, gently tell yourself, "It's okay. I can be kind to myself about this situation. I'm choosing to live the wellbeing way."

Even if you've developed a negative habit of beating yourself up with your thoughts, you can shift your self-talk to positive self-talk. Adding self-kindness to your daily routine shifts your energy and positively impacts how you feel as you move through your day.

When you practise talking kindly to yourself, you build your self-kindness muscle, and you feel better. The cherry on the top is, the kinder you are to yourself, the kinder you'll be to others, and what you give out, you get back.

8

The Reaching for Relief Tool

Acknowledging and accepting how you feel moment-to-moment, every day, is the foundation for strong emotional wellbeing. Feelings are your conscious mental awareness, state or reaction. Emotions are your personalised, in-built guidance system, and tuning into them is a brilliant wellbeing tool.

At first, this can be challenging, even confronting, especially if you've never really thought about your daily feelings and emotions or if you've spent most of your life avoiding them. (And if you've completed the Wellbeing Reflection Activity at the back of the book, you'll know what I mean.)

A friend once said to me, "When I pour myself a glass of wine, I feel as though I'm reaching for relief." In that moment, I loved her openness, and I could totally relate. In my teens, I'd binge drink as a way of escaping my self-loathing, and although I didn't realise it at the time, I too was reaching for relief.

This self-sabotaging habit lasted into my early twenties. I was an all-or-nothing drinker, and the alcohol combined with a lack of self-love was a totally toxic mix. My drinking exacerbated my self-loathing, and I'd project this feeling onto those around me. Drinking for relief was a habit I needed to change.

Around age twenty-four, I learnt about emotional wellbeing. Up until that time, I hadn't been aware of it and therefore didn't know how to navigate my feelings and emotions, which is another reason why I'm passionate about teaching children how to build emotional resilience.

In 2017, I decided to go 365 days without an alcoholic drink. Over the previous decade, I'd been a more conscious drinker, though the memory of how I used to abuse alcohol made me curious to see how I could manage my feelings and emotions without it. I wanted to know that no matter what challenges arose, I had the power within me to navigate them without reaching for relief by having a drink.

Do I still have the occasional drink? Yes. However, I no longer use alcohol as an escape. I simply choose to have a drink because I enjoy a glass of red wine with my hubby over dinner or an espresso martini with my friends.

What matters most is the intention behind why you choose to do something. You always know the difference between healthy and unhealthy habits; ask yourself, "Am I making a conscious choice right now, or am I reaching for relief?"

I want to emphasise that reaching for relief isn't the same as the occasional celebratory drink. Pouring yourself a glass of wine on a Friday night after a hectic week while cooking dinner for the family is a perfect example of a little mum-treat; you shouldn't feel guilty about treating yourself every now and then.

Thinking about our feelings and emotions can make us feel uncomfortable, and often, our first reaction is to push them away or pretend they don't exist. I blocked out my emotions by choosing to have a drink; however, others may do so by overeating, obsessively exercising, working long hours, using drugs, blaming others, gossiping, playing the victim, or making excuses.

It takes courage to be completely honest with yourself, and the power in doing so is incredible. Once you gain clarity on how you feel, the freedom you'll feel is empowering. Anything becomes possible.

Shining a light on how you feel is the first step in building your emotional intelligence. The mere action of feeling your feelings and emotions is one of the best wellbeing actions you can take. Remember, all feelings and emotions are beneficial, as they are our inner guidance. However, some feelings and emotions simply feel better than others, and therefore we label them positive or negative.

Inspired Action, Part One: Take a moment to think about and write down all the feelings and emotions you've felt over the past few days. Place them into two columns, headed "Negative" and "Positive." Place the ones that feel good in the Positive column, and place the ones that don't feel good in the Negative column.

For one minute, look over your list (without judgement) and simply accept that you're beautifully human and have experienced a range of feelings and emotions over the past few days. It's okay and absolutely normal to experience a plethora of feelings and emotions in any one day.

Inspired Action, Part Two: Circle three positive feelings or emotions on your list that you would like to develop over the coming week. If you didn't have any to circle, write down three that you would like to feel in your everyday life.

Inspired Action, Part Three: Decide to take one small action now that will help you cultivate one of the positive feelings or emotions. For example, if you wish to cultivate ease, one action you can take is to ask yourself, "Will this matter in a few weeks, a few months, or a few years?" This will help put things into perspective, as you respond to various situations that arise throughout the day. In many cases, the answer to this question will be, "No, not really." Therefore, you won't need to react negatively, and you'll simply be able to work towards feeling the positive feeling or emotion that you desire.

Your reactions are often overreactions to events, behaviours, or situations that you experience. By adopting a slightly more easy-going attitude (by taking simple actions), you will invite more ease into your day.

How you feel and respond to your feelings and emotions helps determine your emotional wellbeing, and your emotional wellbeing matters a lot. How you feel impacts how you perceive, experience, and interpret your relationships and experiences in your life.

When you become the master of your emotional wellbeing, you'll feel more successful in all that you do and are less likely to reach for relief. Feeling emotionally resilient (which is different from emotionless) gives you the confidence to know that you can manage whatever life throws your way. You'll have authentic emotional power and feel more self-assured each day, and what a wonderful way to strengthen your wellbeing.

9

The Guilt-Free Guide to Better Wellbeing Tool

Guilt, like other negative emotions, is an indication that your wellbeing is out of alignment. If you're experiencing guilt of any sort, celebrate your awareness of it. How guilt looks, feels, and plays out is different for everyone, and only you'll know how best to get your wellbeing back on track. The tools in this book can help.

Use guilt as your first step to getting your wellbeing into alignment. Noticing when you're feeling guilty is key, as it can become a habit. Like worrying, guilt can make you feel like you're doing something about your situation; however, it has no benefits in the long term. If and when you're aware of it, remember to use guilt only to get your wellbeing back on track.

A little while ago, I took on a work contract that looked amazing on paper, but as I began the job, my wellbeing began to suffer, and I was struggling. As a result, I was getting frustrated over things that usually wouldn't worry me. I was arguing with my husband (over silly things) and even snapped at a family member whose energy wasn't great, but because my energy was down too, we clashed.

I believe my happiness is my responsibility, and I was feeling upset that I put myself in that position, as well as guilty for not being my best at work or at home.

The final straw came when I was driving with my son, and I spoke unkindly to him. Jonathan turned and said to me, "Mum, what's going on with you? You don't seem as happy as you usually are."

Ouch, like a slap in the face, he had just verbalised how I'd been feeling for the past few weeks, and he was so right. I told him I was sorry and that I'd been doing some work I disliked. I felt stuck but promised him I'd make changes so that I'd be back on track quickly.

I felt guilty that I hadn't been living my values due to fear; after my lung collapse, I promised myself I'd never do that again. The next day, I emailed the person in charge of the contract and said I'd be finishing up after the next session. It was tough, but my happiness and my family's happiness weren't worth jeopardising. I felt instant relief and knew I had made the best decision, not only for me but for my family too.

Inspired Action: When you feel the emotion of guilt within you, pause and acknowledge it. Then get curious about why you're feeling guilty. Ask yourself, "Why am I feeling guilty now? What thoughts have I been thinking? What is one action I can take to help me feel more at ease in this moment?"

By being totally honest, you'll reveal why you feel the way you do. Clarity is powerful. When you begin self-exploring, you may realise you haven't spent enough time on your wellbeing; in fact, you may feel depleted. This often leads to negative emotions such as exhaustion, stress, anxiety, and guilt.

Inspired Action: Take a moment to schedule five minutes of replenishment time. This may be reading a few pages from the book you've been trying to get to or sitting outside in your garden.

Your rejuvenation time is essential, and it won't happen unless you schedule it in. You spend so much of your time doing things for others that your wellbeing needs are being pushed to the bottom of your priority list. Consistently ignoring your self-care will lead to exhaustion. Refusing to give yourself permission can be soul-destroying in the long term. Needing to replenish yourself is absolutely okay. It's natural to need rejuvenation (just like filling up your car with fuel) because when you take the time to do this, not only do you benefit, but so do all those around you.

10

The Powerful Pause Tool

The power of a simple pause is huge. It can often determine whether you say something kind or say something hurtful. Your words matter. They wield power. By simply pausing before you speak, you give yourself the opportunity to respond calmly rather than react hastily.

The difference between reacting and responding is bigger than you think. A reaction is quick and from a place of pain or fear. A response is calm and thoughtful. It only takes a couple of seconds to check in with yourself before responding to any situation, and by doing so, you master the art of responding.

I can recall a situation that left me completely exhausted. I'd stayed up too late a few nights in a row to meet a deadline. This meant that I chose to sleep an extra thirty minutes in the morning rather than exercise. When Jonathan started complaining about not wanting to go to school, my immediate reaction was to mumble, "Seriously, you think you have a hard life?"

I wasn't being compassionate at all. Luckily, I caught myself doing this. I took a deep breath, knowing I could be conscious of my feelings, and responded with as much kindness as I could muster. It wasn't his fault that I'd stayed up late and felt tired and grumpy, and it was my responsibility not to project my feelings onto him. The powerful pause in this situation was a blessing.

Examples

No Pause	After a Powerful Pause
I'm busy right now.	Let's schedule in some time together.
How many times have I told you?	Can we chat about what's happening here?
Get out.	I just need a minute.
Are you serious?	Wow, I'm surprised about that.
No.	Can we discuss this tonight?
You're annoying me.	I'm feeling frustrated at the moment.
I haven't got time to listen now.	I'd like to hear more about that.

| Oh, for goodness sake. | What do you need right now? |
| Why don't you just do what you've been told? | How can I help you with this? |

Inspired Action: No matter what the situation might be, before responding to your child today, take one slow, deep breath and check in with yourself to see how you are feeling. It's especially important to catch yourself when you're feeling out of sorts so that you become aware and choose not to take whatever you're feeling out on your child. This is what I like to call Conscious Parenting 101: becoming aware of how you feel and taking responsibility for it.

The powerful pause is a key wellbeing tool. The more you remember to pause, the higher your emotional wellbeing will be and the happier you will feel, which will have a positive impact on those in your home. You'll be less likely to blame, criticise, or be unkind. Taking a couple of seconds to check in with yourself helps you to be mindful of how you're feeling.

Recognising how you feel in the moment helps you rethink your reaction and gives you the opportunity to respond more consciously. It helps you preserve the beautiful connection you have with your child. Connection is everything, and what we say and how we say it matters—a lot.

11

The Don't Take It Personally Tool

I've been talking to myself kindly for a decade now, and I still have to remain vigilant of my thoughts and be mindful of what I allow myself to focus on throughout the day.

Self-kindness and maintaining your mental wellbeing are ongoing processes, every day. Whenever you're thinking or speaking, you're always coming from either a love-based mindset or a fear-based mindset. Tuning in to your feelings helps you to know which mode you're in at any given time.

Fear can be a sneaky, unwanted intruder. Its job is to protect you, but sometimes, it goes too far and ends up hurting you. You must be mindful of your feelings in order to catch a fear-based mindset when it starts to creep in.

One time, it took me a couple of days to notice that I had slipped into a fear-based mindset. I caught myself asking, "Why aren't you more compassionate, Rhiannon? Why does this worry you so much? Did you actually do something to upset them?" All of which was far from a love-based mindset; nevertheless, this was where my mind was at the time.

One of my loved ones who has had bipolar depression her whole life was experiencing a really long down period. We speak regularly and know a lot about what's going on in each other's world; however, after six weeks of engaging in only quick (and dismissive) chats, I started to feel like I'd done something wrong. I was taking it personally. My rational brain knew this wasn't the case because from past experience, withdrawal and avoidance was the way her depression manifested. However, my irrational, fear-based mindset started to take over. After trying the acceptance approach (always being there; offering a happiness gift; and calling to check in), I got fed up and, worst of all, started to give my power away. Fear and resentment had crept in, and I wasn't coming from a love-based mindset. It turned out my loved one was struggling to manage a different stage of life and had stopped taking her medication without consulting a doctor. So you never know the struggles someone is going through (even when you know them really well), and it's usually not about you. So it's important not to take their behaviour or actions to heart.

Inspired Action: Decide not to take things personally, even when it feels like it's personal. When you catch yourself in a fear-based mindset or asking yourself fear-based questions, pause, and remind yourself that it's not about you; it's okay to give yourself and others a break. You can choose which mindset you use to engage with the world in any given moment.

You're in charge of you. No one else has the power to derail your wellbeing, unless you allow them. We're surrounded by so many people who have ongoing personal battles; some we are aware of, some we are not. What's truly important is that no matter what, we don't make another person's story, challenge, or drama about us. It really isn't about us; it's 100 percent about them, and only they have the power to change it.

It's a fine line between being there for somebody and not being pulled into their challenge. That is why not taking it personally is such a valuable wellbeing tool. You can interpret their actions from a love-based mindset or a fear-based mindset. The stories, the questions, the comments in your head about what that other person is doing are simply your interpretations. The power of focus is within you, and your focus is up to you.

12

The Make Time to Meditate Tool

This wellbeing tool is incredibly important. You might be reading this and thinking, *Yeah, yeah, what difference will meditating make?* I used to think that too, but it really does make a massive difference to how you feel. In fact, I believe it's an absolute necessity for you if you wish to boost your emotional wellbeing.

When I first started meditating, I wasn't very dedicated. I would do it one day and not the next. However, I'd heard my favourite teachers such as Eckhart Tolle, Oprah, Shefali Tsabary, Esther Hicks, Gabby Bernstein, and Wayne Dyer discuss the power of being consistent with your meditation and decided it was time to give it a proper go. And like many things, until you give it a go yourself, only then do you truly feel the difference it makes.

I noticed that whenever I made time to meditate, my day would flow with ease, and I'd feel so much calmer. Why? Because I had primed my wellbeing muscle. I've been meditating for eight years now, and it has transformed my wellbeing. I can't imagine my life without it. My emotions used to be all over the shop, up, down, and all around. In fact, in my early twenties, I felt like I was losing my mind. I remember calling my mum and saying to her, "I think I'm going crazy." My emotions were controlling me. I felt overwhelmed and didn't know how to self-soothe.

Meditation is the emotional grounding tool that I'd been seeking for so many years. If you wish to feel more emotionally grounded every day, this tool is for you.

As this tool is so powerful, I've included a two-part inspired action. I suggest beginning with the meditation shower and notice how this feels. When you're ready to take your practice a step further, you can create your twenty-one-day meditation plan.

Inspired Action, Part One: Make time for a meditation shower. When you step into the shower, take eight deep breaths. Be fully present while you're standing there; enjoy the feeling of the water, and focus on your breath. If you haven't set the tone for your day, you may decide to do your Positive Action Plan tool during your meditation shower.

When your thoughts wander to conversations that happened yesterday or events that are happening later in the week, gently bring your focus back to how the water feels.

Spending a few present moments in the shower preparing for the day is a powerful wellbeing tool. It doesn't take any extra time, but it transforms ordinary shower time into magical me time. This is the perfect way to incorporate meditation into your mornings.

Inspired Action, Part Two: Create a twenty-one-day meditation plan.

Week One: Commit to sitting and breathing for three minutes each morning for seven days. Make it a non-negotiable part of your morning routine. A great time to do this is straight after you've created your Positive Action Plan.

Week Two: Increase your sitting time to six minutes. Focus on the sounds around you; it could be the morning birds outside your window, soft music, the dogs barking, or even passing traffic. As you sit and become aware of your surroundings, take slow, deep breaths.

Week Three: Extend your sitting time to twelve minutes. At the end of each meditation, remind yourself of your intentions and priorities for the day.

Note: I know some days are crazy, so I understand how challenging this tool may feel in the beginning. However, by making meditation a priority, you'll transform your wellbeing and ride the daily chaos with more grace, ease, and clarity. Consistency is essential. And it gets easier as your children grow. When I first began, they'd be crawling all over me whilst I was trying to sit and breathe (they don't anymore).

Once you decide to meditate each day, continue to do so until it becomes a habit. If, on any given day, three, six, or twelve minutes seems overwhelming, simply sit and breathe for one minute.

There are still days that I only manage a few minutes of meditation, but no matter what, I honour myself and my meditation practise by sitting and breathing before going out into the world. I hope you decide to do this for yourself too.

13

The Relationship Architect Tool

Up until I was twenty-eight, I was living my first life. I was cruising by on autopilot, going through the daily motions, and essentially living life half-heartedly. This way of living isn't uncommon and might feel like a safe choice; however, it's a dissatisfying way to use your time.

Deciding to really start living was a huge wellbeing turning point. For you, it may come after a life-changing event, as it did for me. My total lung collapse was the universe's way of telling me to wake up and really start living. This was my experience; you certainly don't have to wait for a wake-up event in order to live your life fully. This isn't a trial run; you can decide to live whole-heartedly right now.

Your relationships play a significant role in how you experience life. Your social wellbeing matters and will tell you if you're engaging positively with the people in your life (or not). When your relationships are easy and in flow, you're thriving and in wellbeing alignment.

Ten years prior to writing this book, I did a social inventory. This meant shining a light on all the relationships in my life. That included the relationship with my partner; the relationships with my friends, my family, and my workmates; and my interactions with the wider community. This was a daunting task; however, I knew if I wanted to elevate my wellbeing, a good place to start was during my daily interactions with my loved ones. Remember that clarity is wellbeing gold.

Inspired Action, Part One: Complete a social inventory.

Write down all the people in your life. Begin with those in your home, then move onto your extended family, friends, co-workers, and any local community members that you see regularly such as your child's kinder teacher, local barista, or school mums.

Beside each name on your list, write a brief summary of the relationship. You may even like to give each one a score out of 10, a 10 being "mostly brilliant interactions" and a 0 being "mostly negative interactions."

Take a moment to look over your list and think about which relationships in your life need some positive attention. Where could you give more of your unconditional love?

Inspired Action, Part Two: Make a note of one person who deserves more of your unconditional love. Decide on one action you can take today to see only the good or appreciate that person on a deeper level. This tiny shift will most certainly impact your next interaction with her or him. Notice how the energy has shifted and how you may even elicit a different response. You're becoming a relationship architect.

By deciding to fully engage with those around you, you'll deepen your relationship with them and simultaneously boost your own wellbeing too. It's a wellbeing win–win.

14

The Family Bubble Tool

Your family bubble consists of those gorgeous humans who live with you in your home. Your family bubble is precious and needs to be nurtured each and every day.

It can be easy to get caught up in the "take loved ones for granted" way of living; however, you don't have to continue operating in autopilot mode.

To successfully nurture your family bubble, you need to nurture yourself first. Having a daily nurturing plan is essential. Once you have this in place, you'll be able to give to your loved ones consistently without feeling burnt out or depleted. Little things, like playing a game or taking a family walk, are simple ways to connect and spend quality time together.

Now, I must be totally honest: I'm not a natural cook. It's never been a passion of mine, and when I left home, I had no idea how to even boil an egg. However, I love connecting over a meal with my family. To me, it's a special time. While I always try to make the dinners healthy and interesting, my main priority is focussed on creating positive energy around the table. I want our dinner table to be a place of happiness, good old-fashioned chats, and lots of laughter. Sometimes, we use this time to share our challenges and celebrations; it's one way we stay connected. We have a "No technology at the dinner time" rule, which we started while the kids were young, so they're used to it and don't push back on it (well, not yet, anyway).

Inspired Action: Ask yourself, "What does my family bubble need most right now?"

Lovingly observe those in your home. How are they doing? Is there anything you feel they need from you? How could you create some more family time together? You may feel your family bubble is going along okay, and they simply need your continued presence and kindness. You may also feel that they're going through a challenging time and need extra reassurance, support, or special attention. If your observations don't reveal a lot to you, ask them, "What do you need from me right now?"

A happy family bubble is priceless. When you prioritise nurturing your family bubble, you'll make better daily choices. You'll soon know if a choice you make nurtures your family bubble or not. You feel it energetically.

Remember, small moments of kindness matter. A loving smile, a hug, a game, a walk, a family meal, or some slow time together is often all that's needed to nurture the family bubble.

15

The It's Okay to Say No Tool

It's absolutely okay to say no. And to be honest, in order for your wellbeing to thrive, it's an essential word to have in your self-care vocabulary.

No matter how hard you try, you can't be everything or do everything for everyone. Your hesitation (or refusal) to say no may stem from a desire to please. Sooner or later, you can be sure that not saying no will very quickly deplete your wellbeing.

Many requests are small and are asked by friends and loved ones, which can make it harder to say no. However, all of these small requests add up and can be quite time-consuming.

Sometimes, we fear saying no because we worry we won't be liked or we might be judged. Here's a tip: surround yourself with people who accept you no matter what.

Your family and friends may have come to always expect a yes from you for every request. And now that you're prioritising yourself and aren't willing to jeopardise your wellbeing in order to please others, saying no can be challenging. Your loving family members and most of your true friends will still love and respect you, even if you say no (and even if they're put out by your choice).

Ask yourself, "What's the best wellbeing choice that I can make for myself right now?"

I've found myself in these situations many times, and I'd like to share one with you. My family and I were invited to my cousin's daughter's first birthday party. I initially replied yes, but when the day of the party arrived, I didn't feel up to it. Quite simply, I was exhausted. I had my second throat infection that month and knew that what I needed most was to lay low and rest. I would visit my cousin and her daughter another time. I called her to explain why we wouldn't be there. I was honest, and she understood, as she also prioritises her wellbeing.

However, I know it's not that simple for everyone. Sometimes, family members expect you to always be at every event and ask you why you're not. If this happens, you may take the opportunity to share your current priorities and needs. You may choose to tell them that your own family needs you right now or that you're feeling run down and need time to rest. Realistically, it's their choice how they respond, but it's up to you to not take their response personally. I know this can be difficult (especially the first time), which is why Tool 26 really comes in handy: the Care Less about What Others Think tool. It will help you put yourself first.

Inspired Action: Next time you receive any type of request, take the time to pause and reflect on the following questions:

- Am I currently on top of or overwhelmed by my to-do list?
- Does this feel like a good wellbeing choice for me?
- How will this request impact my wellbeing?
- Is this request in alignment with my family wellbeing goals and values?

It's possible to say a positive no (that is without guilt, worry, or explanation). However, if you think you might struggle to say a simple, "No, thank you," try an alternative, such as, "I'd love to help, but unfortunately, I can't take on any more commitments right now." If it's something you'd like to help out with in the future, don't be afraid to say so. Your friend, loved one, or colleague will appreciate your honesty, just as you would appreciate their honesty if the situation was reversed.

It's futile trying to bend yourself every which way in order to please those around you; it's nearly impossible and definitely not sustainable. Schedule in what's important to you first, and make time for your priorities. Everything else is extra, so as each request arises, take time to consider each one from your wellbeing's perspective, using the above questions as a guide.

If you take on too much, overcommit, or aim to please everyone, your wellbeing will diminish. Remember, "No," is a complete sentence.

16

The Toxic Thought Detox Tool

Your mental wellbeing needs to be high on your priority list. You may feel you have little control over which thoughts enter your mind, but you do have the power to decide which ones you dwell on and which ones you let go.

Your thoughts matter a lot. Your thoughts fuel your perceptions, which fuel your emotions, which fuel your behaviours and actions.

According to best-selling author, Dr Joe Dispenza, on any one day, we have around seventy thousand thoughts, with many being exactly the same as the day before. These thoughts create our perception of what we experience, and therefore, we don't perceive what we see; we actually see what we perceive.

So many of our thoughts are habitual (and often negative); they run wild on autopilot day after day, remaining active in our minds. This is something you can change. It simply takes a little willingness and focus. Will it be easy? Initially, probably not, as it will feel uncomfortable and unfamiliar. But when you step out of your comfort zone with the intention to rewire your thoughts, it's so worth the effort.

Inspired Action, Part One: To maintain good mental wellbeing, become conscious of your thoughts. Notice which thoughts you tend to dwell on; are they negative or positive?

After my lung collapse back in 2009, I spent almost two weeks in hospital recovering. During that time, I read Eckhart Tolle's book *A New Earth,* and it changed my life forever. From the moment I left the hospital, I lived differently. I finally understood that my thoughts weren't me. I was me, and my thoughts were merely passing through me. I could observe them without judgement. I became detached from my thoughts, and they no longer controlled me. For the first time in my life, I felt free. It was exhilarating. And the best part is that once you know this, you can never go back. At times, you may forget this way of living and feel awful, but you'll know how to go back to being the observer of your thoughts. This is true wellbeing power.

Ask yourself, "Do I observe my thoughts as they arise, or do I react to them?"

Inspired Action, Part Two: Catch a negative thought, and tweak it into a positive one. For example, a negative thought might be, *I'm always so busy; I never have any time to myself.* Catch it and tweak it to create a positive version: *I have a lot on today, but I've got time to spend a few minutes doing something I enjoy.* Once you recognise which thoughts are detracting from your mental wellbeing, you're perfectly positioned to catch and reverse negative thought patterns.

Beauty emanates from within, and it begins in your mind. When you perceive your thoughts with love and choose to dwell on the positive ones, your energy shifts, and your wellbeing rises to new heights.

17

The Let It Go Tool

This tool is all about sharing the gift of forgiveness with yourself and others. Opening yourself up to forgiveness helps you to live your best life, every day. Forgiveness is the highest form of self-love.

Forgiveness is an essential part of nurturing your wellbeing. It's a mindset, and it's about you. Forgiveness releases past hurts (without condoning them) so that you no longer have to carry them with you. Forgiveness is the mental letting go of the toxic bonds that you have with another person (or with yourself).

It's about wiping the slate clean and making a fresh start. Non-forgiveness is toxic. It keeps you stuck in a cloud of negativity and stops you from embracing your inner power, beauty, and authenticity.

I started my forgiveness journey at age twenty-eight, and it was one of the hardest things I've ever had to do. Before this time, I was the queen of holding grudges. It was a scary and vulnerable road into the unknown, but I'm so happy I was brave enough to begin. And I know you will be too.

I began with forgiving myself for not loving me, for not knowing my worth, and for not knowing my value. What I now know is that my negative attitude and behaviour came from not loving myself enough. I had to forgive myself for self-sabotaging and for my low self-worth. I was my own worst enemy. There were lots of things I had to forgive myself for, such as staying in a toxic relationship, drinking too much (especially the time I knocked myself out after falling over and waking up in hospital with stitches above my eyebrow), treating my husband with unkindness, the physical fight I had with my sister, and yelling at my loved ones—all because I didn't have enough self-love.

Next, I chose to forgive all the people in my life who I felt had wronged me. And oh boy, this list was long. Nevertheless, I started, and it was one of the best things I've ever done. It helped me to start again. I started fresh. I felt free. It was a new beginning.

Forgiveness makes space for positive energy to infuse your world. The more you're willing to release built-up resentment, the lighter and more peaceful you'll feel.

In order to forgive, you first need to be willing, and this choice creates a beautiful ripple effect. Once you begin to forgive, watch in awe how certain people and the right things show up in order to support your journey.

Inspired Action: Decide that you want inner peace and decide to let it go and be willing to forgive. When you're willing to forgive yourself and others for all past hurts, you're well on your way to embracing the beauty of forgiveness. Willingness is Step 1 in my Five Steps to Forgiveness.

These are the Five Steps to Forgiveness:

1. Willingness
2. Forgiveness Reflection
3. Forgiveness Inventory
4. Acknowledge and Release
5. Morning Blessings

If you're interested in learning about the Five Steps to Forgiveness, you'll find this life-changing process at the back of the book.

By choosing to forgive freely, you instantly begin to feel lighter and more at peace with life. Once you embrace forgiveness, the energy shift that takes place within you is so powerful that it'll leave an imprint on your heart forever. Everyone in your life will feel the shift too, and they'll be truly grateful that you decided to forgive and let it go.

To forgive someone else, you don't need an apology. You may never receive one. It's simply a choice about self-love. Remember, forgiveness is about you, not them. Decide to love yourself enough to begin your forgiveness journey today.

18

The Positive Conversation Tool

It's not difficult to become a master of positive chat. Having short, wellbeing-focused conversations are powerful because they uplift your mood instantly and help the person you're speaking with feel uplifted too.

You'll know when you've engaged in a positive conversation when you walk away feeling good rather than depleted. This doesn't mean you don't share your challenges with others; it just means there's a time and a place to do so. Choose a good friend to chat with in a way that is meaningful and with perspective; it's time well spent. It's wonderful to feel comfortable enough to share your challenges, but when you're talking about challenges too often, you not only deplete your wellbeing but you drain the energy of those (often unsuspecting) people too.

I absolutely understand that when you're going through a difficult time, it can be tough getting out of bed, let alone entering the schoolyard to pick up your child. With this in mind, why not take the opportunity to elevate your wellbeing by connecting with others through fun, light-hearted conversations?

Inspired Action, Part One: Begin your conversations with a positive comment or story, and watch how positivity gains momentum and attracts more of the same.

Here's an example: For the few minutes that you chat with another mum, perhaps at school drop-off or pick-up, make it your intention to talk about something positive that's happening in your life. Ultimately, you never really know what's going on in someone's life, which is why it's important to remember that almost everyone is managing some sort of challenge. A little positive conversation goes a long way.

If you feel like you need to talk to someone, be proactive and ask a mum (or a few) to meet with you. Feeling connected and knowing that you're not alone are essential elements of your long-term happiness.

Sharing (with perspective) in a safe environment became so valuable to me back in 2015 that it inspired my first mum's wellbeing circle. I created a comfortable space where mums could share and discuss their challenges and celebrations in a private setting. We're all on this motherhood journey together, and surrounding myself with like-minded mums has been was one of my best wellbeing choices to date.

Inspired Action, Part Two: Decide to begin your own wellbeing circle. Invite a group of mums to meet regularly in a relaxed space to discuss your motherhood challenges and celebrations. This way, you have time to be there for one another and support each other in a meaningful way.

I know that some days are really tough, and you'll find it challenging to be part of positive conversations, let alone negative ones. And when you find yourself being depleted by negative chat, politely excuse yourself and go to the bathroom; disengage by not saying too much in return; change the subject; or find a friend who is willing to have a light-hearted chat with you. You don't have to stay there; be proactive and move, because nurturing your wellbeing is your priority.

Making positive conversations a priority will transform your relationships. It'll draw those who are on your wellbeing path closer and naturally distance those who aren't, because like attracts like.

When in doubt, ensure that you have more positive conversations in a day than negative ones. Be there for others when you can, and when you're having a tough day, be proactive and decide to prioritise you.

19

The Make Time to Move Your Body Tool

Making time to move your body regularly is such an important wellbeing tool. The research around moving your body is undeniable; physical movement releases feel-good chemicals called endorphins, which naturally boost your mood. As a mum, making time to move your body (that doesn't include running errands) is wellbeing gold.

The great thing about this tool is that it doesn't need to take up a lot of time. Scheduling in time to move your body on a regular basis is so valuable. In no time at all, it'll become a key part of your wellbeing routine, and you'll love it.

Movement doesn't have to be a hassle or become a mundane task. You can make it fun by choosing an activity you enjoy. When I move, I often listen to inspiring podcasts at the same time (I also do this while folding the laundry); you may choose to do this too, or you may prefer to pop on your favourite song and dance to the music as a way of moving your beautiful body.

I like to plan my movement time the night before and often put my runners at the end of the bed, ready to go. When my children were young, I'd wake up multiple times during the night and therefore give myself extra time to sleep in the morning. However, if I'd only been up a couple times for a quick resettle, I knew I could manage adding exercise to my morning routine. You'll learn how to tune in to what you need most for the day ahead. It's important to remember that when your children are young, a little flexibility in your wellbeing routine goes a long way.

Your movement time may be as simple as stretching for five minutes before you have your breakfast or organising a walk with a friend or bopping along to some music with your toddler. It doesn't matter which way you choose to move your body; the key is to schedule it in, and start moving.

If you'd like to supercharge the feel-good chemicals, try making time to move outdoors and enjoy the fresh air. Breathing deeply and observing the natural beauty that surrounds you is an incredible way to boost how you feel.

Inspired Action: Schedule in time this week to move your body. You may do this by yourself or incorporate it as a family outing. Decide to walk, play, stretch, jog, swim, or dance, and watch how your feel-good chemicals soar. Continue to schedule in movement activities that you enjoy. Show your body that you love it and appreciate it by taking care of it. Your body is an amazing gift and helps you do so much in this world. As you move, take time to be in awe of your magnificent body.

Once you notice how good it feels to move your body regularly, you may like to take it to the next level and try a yoga or Pilates class. Feeling good matters, and moving your body is an excellent way to spark your feel-good chemicals into action.

20

The Think Good Thoughts Tool

It's so easy to focus on what you don't want your life to be like; however, what you think about has a way of permeating into your life.

Your wellbeing wishes and desires matter, and when you focus on them, you're more likely to draw them into your life. That's why it's so important to spend time focusing your thoughts on what you want to create more of in your life.

I'm a huge fan of writing down dreams and desires. Visualisations and creating vision boards are fun ways to do this. Your focus is a powerful magnet. A perfect example of is this is my book. I've wanted to create it for over ten years, and my purpose kept me focussed over the 3,653 or so days it has taken me to write. My primary intention was to help mums nurture their wellbeing so they'd be at their best and therefore successfully empower their children to thrive.

Over the years, I thought about giving up. I'd think, *Who am I to write such a book?* or *Is my message really that important?* and then I remembered my intention. I'm writing this for my children, your children, and our children's children. I'm an advocate for all children. Your children need me to share this message, and they need you to listen. Your children may not always be able to say how they feel or ask you to slow down, but they need you to.

Teachers can only do so much in the classroom, and as their mum, you hold the wellbeing power. You can support your children and help them to shine rather than sink. Your children need you to thrive so you can lead the way. Let's start focusing on what you want. Thinking good thoughts is a great way to start.

Inspired Action: Make a list of your wellbeing wishes and desires which, in essence, are your wellbeing goals. Next, write down a few reasons why they're important, as they will help you to stay focussed on your wellbeing wishes and goals.

What's the reason behind your wellbeing desire? Your motivation matters and is the driving force behind your actions. The easiest way to discover your motivation is to ask yourself, "Why?" List your reasons or the motives beneath your wellbeing desires.

For example:

Wellbeing Goal: To feel like I'm a good mum.

Why?

- So I feel successful in what I'm doing
- So my children enjoy their time with me
- So I feel like I'm on the wellbeing track
- So I take responsibility for my life and stop blaming others for how I feel
- So I can sleep well each night, knowing I'm enough
- So I enjoy my life now, not twenty years from now
- So at the end of my day, I have no regrets

Being clear on your motivation makes a huge difference in achieving your wellbeing desires. Your intention helps you remain focussed. Remember, you absolutely deserve to live a happy and fulfilling life now, not at some vague time in the future.

21

The Whole Cup of Tea Tool

Yes, gorgeous mum, I'm talking about sitting down and drinking a whole cup of hot tea in one go. How many times do you make a cuppa and then have a sip, walk away to do something else, and eventually return to your cold cuppa? Well, that baloney ends today. You absolutely deserve at least one hot cuppa every day.

Make your tea time your daily me time. You may even like to create a wellbeing mantra to go with it. My favourite tea time mantra is, "Tea time is me time."

A friend recently said to me, "I'm so busy, I don't even have time for a cuppa."

I get it. I used to prioritise always being on the move too, so I asked my friend if she had time to be sick or exhausted. She of course told me she didn't. I suggested she try making some time during her daily routine to have a mini break, such as stopping to enjoy a whole cup of tea.

She was still not convinced that this would make a difference, so I told her to think of it like this: Rather than go, go, go, stop from exhaustion, and take days to recover, try go, go, go, break for a cup of tea, and get some energy back as you make your way through your to-do list.

A week later, after trying my suggestion, she called to say how amazed she was that stopping for a cuppa actually helped her elevate her energy and feel more productive.

Inspired Action: Make yourself a cup of tea. Sit down and enjoy it until you see the bottom of the cup while it's still hot. As you're sitting down with your warm cup of tea, remind yourself of how your wellbeing matters. This would also be a wonderful time for your mantra, "Tea time is me time," acknowledging that taking time for yourself is a nurturing wellbeing action. You deserve to nurture yourself every day.

Making time for you each day is essential if you want to feel good consistently. You can no longer hold busyness up on a pedestal. Busyness doesn't equal your self-worth.

Years ago, I had a busyness epiphany. I was having a latte with an old friend when our conversation turned into a busy-off. She was telling me how much she had on her to-do list, and then I told her all the things I was doing;

it was like a competition. Who would win the busy-off title?

In that moment, I dropped my need to be busy and decided that I'd no longer use busyness as a badge of honour. In fact, I rarely use the word *busy* now when I talk.

The way you talk about your time matters, and it impacts how you feel about your time. If you want to feel good about your time, you need to talk about it positively.

You'll always make time to do a load of washing or put away the clothes; however, if you never schedule in time for a hot cuppa, you may never actually have one. How you use your time matters. My rule of thumb is, hot cuppa first, load of washing second. By scheduling in time for yourself, you prioritise *you* without putting your wellbeing off until you get everything done. If you're anything like me, my washing is never done, and if I waited until I finished my daily tasks before I sat down, I'd never sit down.

22

The Rest and Recharge Tool

"I don't have time to rest; there is always so much to do," is something I hear all too often from mums. To which I respond, "Do you have time to feel emotionally and physically drained?"

Being a mum, you're probably used to being on the go and usually only stop if you're forced to, perhaps due to an awful cold, sheer exhaustion, or when a huge wake-up call comes along.

I understand. I used to live my life like this. Fast paced, always on the go. I had the mentality that resting meant lazy. This is not the way I feel about rest now. I think it's essential to live at your best each day. When my children weren't sleeping and I was running on empty, the dishes didn't get done until they were needed. I didn't clean the house for weeks, and the washing pile was enormous. These tasks simply weren't the priority. When my beautiful mum would come over and start doing the dishes, I'd tell her that they weren't the priority, even though I was grateful I had someone to help.

I knew if I'd forced myself to do the dishes while trying to be present and interact with my children, I'd have become the stressed-out and yelling mum that I didn't want to be. I chose to lay low, play with the children, and not worry about the dishes. I knew that I'd never look back on those years and feel glad I did the dishes diligently. Instead, I look back and am so glad I prioritised rest and play with my children when they were young. This can be challenging because it goes against the status quo. However, after returning to the school environment, I know more than ever that our children need us to slow down, rest, play, and prioritise time with them. Their wellbeing, happiness, and academic success depend on it.

If you feel really stretched with your time or work long hours in an office while the children are really young, it's about maximising your time when you're home. Think quality. It's not necessarily about the amount of time you spend resting and recharging; it's more about the quality and consistency of it.

For example, if you worked a ten-hour day and need to prepare dinner when you get home, prioritise a short rest time with your little one before you begin. Take ten minutes to snuggle up on the couch together and read a book. This ticks so many wellbeing boxes for the both of you. You get to stop and reset before starting the evening routine, and your child gets quality time with you. They know they matter to you because you spent time with them before jumping straight into the night routine. In fact, research suggests that reading out aloud to your child accelerates their oral language and brain development, therefore setting them up for literacy success. Keep in mind that this isn't always easy to do, and sometimes, it won't happen. However, prioritising this time, surrendering to the moment, being fully present, and focusing on what is happening right there (not on the tasks you still have to do before you go to bed) will recharge you (and your little one) for the night ahead.

Don't wait to rest; schedule in regular rest periods now. I hear mums say, "I'll rest once I've done all the chores," or "I'll rest once I'm on holidays at the end of the year."

Oh. My. Goodness. Putting off rest and rejuvenation is like saying you'll fill up the car with petrol at Christmas time (and run on empty until then). Regular rest matters and makes a huge difference in how you feel on a daily basis.

Inspired Action: Take out your calendar and mark in two fifteen-minute breaks this week labelled "My rest time." Then, most importantly, commit to taking them. It may mean a bath once the children are asleep, or listening to some quiet music while you lay down, or reading a chapter of a book you've been wanting to start.

Rest helps you to maintain your wellbeing and reset it regularly. By making rest part of your weekly routine, you'll feel more energised as you tend to the myriad tasks that you have on your mum plate.

23

The Unwavering Belief in Yourself Tool

You know yourself better than anyone, and after going through some of these wellbeing tools and processes, it's highly likely that you now know yourself a little better than before.

Being your own best friend is essential for your wellbeing journey, and it begins with a decision to be your own best supporter.

There's only one person who truly knows what makes you happy, knows what your heart desires most, knows the amazing things you're capable of achieving, and knows what fulfils you. That person is you.

My wish for you is that you develop an unwavering faith in your ability to do your best and live the life you truly desire, on your terms.

Developing unwavering self-belief is something I'm especially passionate about because if I didn't have strong faith in myself and in my ability to achieve my goals, I'd never have written this book. For many years, I've known that I wanted to share my wellbeing tools in the form of a book (and I'm absolutely thrilled beyond belief that it's now a reality).

However, in the lead-up to achieving this dream, I had a beautiful, well-meaning person in my life (who loves me) share with me her honest opinion about my goal, asking, "Who is actually going to read your book?" I didn't say much in response to what she'd said, and while I thanked her for her opinion, I didn't for one moment take it to heart. I just knew that many mums would read my book.

You see, if I didn't have unwavering self-belief in my message and in my ability to achieve my goal of publishing a book, I would've packed it in after that conversation.

In my heart of hearts, I knew this book was going to be shared with the world and with people like you who are reading it right now! For this, I thank you and I hope my tools are helping you nurture your wellbeing.

Inspired Action: Take some time to really think about what you think about yourself. Do you believe in yourself? Do you allow others to dictate your self-worth?

What would you love to do but don't because you aren't sure what others will think or say? Do you believe you can achieve anything you set your mind to? Write your thoughts down on paper, look them over, and ask yourself if you like what you're reading. If you don't, begin to think about what you can do to make a change and write it down. Repeat this exercise until you feel a shift in how you feel about yourself, until you have unwavering self-belief.

I believe that you can do this, but you need to believe it yourself. You're brilliant and so much stronger than you know; you can achieve your goals, and it begins with a deep knowing, an unwavering belief in yourself that you can have, do, or achieve anything you set your mind and heart to.

24

The Mini-Mum-Tantrum
Acceptance Tool

Like you, I'm human, and some days, I'm much better at riding the daily challenges and chaos of raising young children than others. Yes, these days, my mini-mum-tantrums are few and far between; however, they still occur occasionally. In fact, I had one while writing this book, and I felt it was really important to share it with you.

To set the scene, it's a Friday morning, mid-term in May; it's getting cold here in Australia, and I'm premenstrual. As a family, we're all feeling a little tired, and we've had a lot going on. On top of this, my beautiful ten-year-old son and his attitude are growing by the day. Usually, I can remain present with Jonathan's mood and not buy into his attitude; however, after trying a couple of my wellbeing strategies on this particular morning (breathing a lot, walking away, helping him find his library book in his messy room that I'm now refusing to tidy), I eventually lost it, raised my voice, and said, in a non-loving tone, "Just clean up your room, for goodness sake."

He then proceeded to tell me, "You're not a kind mum, and I'm not cleaning my room because you raised your voice."

Needless to say, the morning wasn't going so well. I'm sharing this with you because mid conversation, my daughter started getting upset and said she didn't like it when I yelled. Thankfully, Madeleine is able to verbalise how she feels (sometimes, children can't, and they internalise their feelings), which encouraged me to pause, be present, and acknowledge my behaviour.

Your actions, behaviours, and words always impact your children. You know this; however, it's something you must hold sacred because how you speak to your children becomes their inner voice and impacts how they interpret the world around them.

Inspired Action: If you find yourself in a similar situation, immediately acknowledge your behaviour, like I did, and try to stop. Apologise, and shift your intention to saving the morning/afternoon/evening as best you can.

After the episode that morning, I apologised, hugged my children, and said, 'I'm really sorry. I was feeling frustrated and made a bad choice. I'm going to take some deep breaths and guide my wellbeing back on track."

When we finally made it to the car, we all took deep breaths and set our intentions for the next part of the day. I apologised again and told the kids I didn't feel good when I raised my voice. I said, "I love you both so much, and I'd appreciate it if we could focus more on teamwork in the morning as we get ready for the day together."

Years ago, I'd have continued to rant, justifying to myself why it was okay that I yelled and offloaded my frustration. These days, I'm much more self-aware and want those around me, especially my children, to feel safe, secure, loved, and happy.

It's important to acknowledge your behaviour, say you're sorry, and appreciate the experience as a wellbeing sign. It simply indicates that you need more replenishment. Using this type of situation as a reminder to fill up your own wellbeing cup is also important. This invaluable insight is one of the most powerful things you can do for yourself and for the wellbeing of your family.

25

The Choose Wellbeing-Minded Friends Tool

Connection is everything. Your social wellbeing is determined by the quality of your relationships. The way you connect, interact, and engage with others greatly impacts your wellbeing because that is how you experience life.

One aspect of social wellbeing that contributes greatly to how you feel each day is your friendships. You may not be able to choose your family; however, you can absolutely choose your friends. You're the one who decides who you spend your time with, and choosing wisely is essential. How you spend your time matters and affects how you feel every day.

When I first became a mum back in 2008, I joined my local mother's group. At that time, none of my friends or family members had young children, so I found it comforting to be surrounded by women who were going through a similar experience. Some days, I was really struggling with lack of sleep. I talked about it with one particular mum from the group who was also experiencing severe sleep deprivation, and it meant the world to me. To know I wasn't alone was powerful and made it easier to manage. We're still friends today, and I'll always appreciate those times when she listened and helped me take a more light-hearted approach to the challenges of raising young children.

Surrounding yourself with kind-hearted, uplifting, authentic individuals who want you to be your best self (who want to be their best self too) is one of the most self-loving gifts.

Friendships often shift depending on what stage of life you are in. So if you're reading these words and thinking that you don't currently have these kinds of friendships, it's okay. New friendships with a focus on wellbeing can begin today.

Inspired Action: Here's where doing a social inventory is important again. Write down a list of your friends on a piece of paper. Circle the friends you enjoy spending time with, the ones who exude positive energy (most of the time), speak positively about others, and focus on positive experiences. Make the decision to keep nurturing these precious friendships. By doing so, you'll be nurturing your own wellbeing, and because you're like-minded, you'll be nurturing theirs too.

Think about acquaintances you could reach out to and see if they'd like to catch up for a coffee. Start looking for a local community group that has members you know share similar interests to you. If you've found someone, or a group of people, who share the same interests online, aim to organise a meet-up in person, as the benefit of an offline connection is powerful.

If you feel your current friendships are not focussed around wellbeing, it's important to remember you may only be coming to this realisation as you've never entertained the idea until now. Before you start to eliminate people you feel don't nurture your wellbeing, try reaching out to your friends with this new perspective, and see if your friendships grow beyond where they are now. While it can be easy and sometimes important to end a friendship, reaching out to a friend with a different perspective and attitude can open up a new dimension in your relationship you never knew existed.

You're the creator of your life, and now is the perfect time to develop positive friendships that will continue on for many years to come. Surround yourself with kind people, and notice how your wellbeing soars to new heights. You deserve the best and deserve to be surrounded by the best too.

26

The Care Less about What Others Think Tool

Motherhood is often rife with judgement, comparison, and criticism, but how would it feel if you started to care less about what others thought of you and cared more about what *you* thought of you?

Focusing on you and what you're doing rather than anyone else is a brilliant wellbeing tool. By keeping your conscious attention on how you feel and what you are thinking, you conserve your precious mental energy, and this helps you stay in wellbeing alignment.

This tiny shift, from external focus to internal focus, changed everything for me. My clarity and inner power skyrocketed, and for the first time, I had control over my opinion of myself.

I know this can be hard, and I absolutely get it because I used to live in fear of what others thought of me, all the time. I didn't trust my inner wisdom and was far more concerned with what others thought of me than with what I thought of myself. I wanted to fit in, be liked and accepted, and be seen as normal, but there was a high price to pay. My spiritual wellbeing was non-existent, and I tried to stay small and safe, so I didn't rock the status quo. Honestly, if my lung had not collapsed, I may not have decided to live life on my terms. But you, lovely mum, don't have to wait for a life-changing moment; you can decide now to live fully for you and in an unabridged way, despite what others think of you.

Inspired Action: Take time to consider how much you care about what others think of you. How do you spend most of your thinking time? Do you think mostly about how others perceive you or about how you think of you?

If you spend more time than you'd like to admit thinking about what others think of you, consider the following questions:

Why do you do this? Are you afraid they won't like you? Do you think they'll disapprove of you or talk negatively about you?

Why are you wondering what they think? Why does this matter to you?

Does your awareness of others impact how you feel about yourself? Does this awareness keep you from trying new things or being authentically you?

And lastly, take some time to notice how *you* feel about yourself.

Sometimes, when we're not feeling confident or strong, we turn our attention outwards for answers, when they can really only be found from within. Know that when you want to focus your attention away from you, it may be a way to distract you from tuning in to yourself. The opinion you have of yourself matters the most, and this is in your hands.

Success is keeping your thoughts focused on you and letting go of what you think others may think of you. When I became conscious of this habit, I was astounded at how much time I spent thinking about what others thought of me. The funny thing about that is, it's such a waste of time. And besides being a total energy zapper, you'll never really know exactly what others think, and it doesn't really matter, anyway; it's just their opinion. Our opinions vary depending on our level of happiness; therefore, the happier we are, the more likely our opinions will be positively infused. Ultimately, the opinions of others say more about how they feel about themselves than you.

This is what matters most: your dreams, your goals, and living your best life. Those who resonate with your way will be there cheering you on, and those who don't, well, they won't. But that's okay because that's their choice, and they may change (or not). Don't spend time thinking about what they think of you, and do your very best to accept and appreciate others just as they are.

Remember, what matters most is your opinion of yourself; when you begin to focus your attention on what others think of you, use this awareness as a wellbeing tool to steer the focus back to you.

27

The Mum-Not-Maid Tool

Keeping a household running is part and parcel of adulthood, and as a parent, it's a never-ending (and often thankless) task to manage. However, that being said, being a mum must always be seen as more than being a maid.

It's possible that in today's fast-paced world, you may've forgotten the true mission of being a mum and allowed society's crazy pace and unrealistic expectations to blur your mission. You must return to the basics of being a mum; your children absolutely need you to.

If you feel like you're a maid (or at risk of becoming one), you can change this now. Keeping a perfect house has never been a priority of mine (and is unlikely ever to be high on my list), but I know things must get done in order to maintain a somewhat smooth-running household. During the days of sleep deprivation, my work took a backseat, and I consciously prioritised the connection with my children before taking care of the household. It wasn't always easy, but looking back, it was such a short time, and I'm so happy I did.

Sometimes, those who love you will find it hard to adjust to your approach. For example, I remember when my children were young, and Nick used to come home from work and glance around the house with the "What have you been doing all day?" look in his eyes. On a few occasions, the house was messier than usual, but I'd simply remind him that the kids were my focus, and I was doing my best. In his defence, he wasn't sleeping well, either, and was having a hard time at work. Being present and compassionate to what he was experiencing stopped me from launching into a list of every single thing I'd done that day. The "Whose Day Was Harder?" game was not one I was willing to play. Keeping a scorecard doesn't cultivate connection, and I wanted better for our relationship.

Inspired Action: Take a few minutes to write down your family wellbeing goals and priorities. Think about what matters most to you and how you'd like to spend your time. This may change weekly or even daily. Forgot about society's expectations: effortlessly running the perfect household while looking like a supermodel and sitting on the board of every committee in the neighbourhood.

Focus on the needs of your family and, of course, your own wellbeing.

Knowing your wellbeing values during the demanding and often blurry times with your children will help you stay on track. The early years are priceless, and you never get them back. Remember, you don't want to look back and regret you didn't give them time each day because you were too busy making sure the house was in perfect order. Your children will adore you for the fun you had with them, not the clean house you kept.

Your mission as a mum is to nurture and lovingly guide your little human beings so they develop and grow into happy, confident, and resilient adults. Those precious minutes will mean the world to them, and as a result, your own wellbeing will soar. To me, this is absolute mothering success.

Remember, the dishes will get done, eventually.

28

The Look for Things to Appreciate Tool

As a mum in the twenty-first century, there are countless things to appreciate; however, we sometimes become so bogged down in the daily grind, we forget to focus on all the good we have in our life.

Appreciation is one of the best wellbeing tools available to us. It's free, it's instantaneous, and once the appreciation momentum takes hold, it can transform how you feel about everything.

I spoke briefly about appreciation in the PAP tool earlier and said how beginning your day with appreciation is a powerful move. When you continue to look for the good and focus on things to appreciate as your day progresses, your wellbeing begins to soar.

In those early years, appreciation was my saving grace. We were under great financial strain, and our renovation budget was blown. I wasn't contributing financially, and we were barely managing to pay the bills and put food on the table. However, knowing the power of appreciation, every day as I'd wake, I'd think how blessed I was to have two healthy children, have my own health intact, and have supportive friends, family, and a hard-working husband.

Inspired Action: Write down ten things that you can appreciate right now. It may include things such as the fresh air you're breathing in, your health, the health of your child, the food in your fridge, the roof over your head, the clean water instantly available, and so on.

After you complete this list, consider sharing it with your family bubble and ask them to join you. Tomorrow, repeat the same activity, and in no time, your appreciation habit will kick in, and you'll automatically look for things to appreciate as you move through your day.

Your daily focus matters so very much. As you go about your daily tasks, take time to notice and soak up all the beautiful colours, smells, and sights that are waiting to be enjoyed. It's impossible to complain at the same time you appreciate the things in your life. However, if you find yourself getting caught up in a moment of difficulty, simply notice where your focus is and switch back into appreciation mode. It's pretty normal to whinge from time to time, but if you want to feel good, aim to spend most of your time in appreciation mode.

Your wellbeing shift from complaining to appreciating will make a huge difference in how you feel each and every day. This is the essence of true wellbeing. How you feel matters. The amazing news is that you can improve how you feel, little by little, and start living your happiest life now. You have the power inside of you; you just have to commit to tuning into it.

29

The Schedule in Parents-Only Time Tool

Raising children and keeping your relationship as parents intact is no easy feat. Almost overnight, you go from having all this time, freedom, and flexibility to being at the beck and call of your precious new family member. It can be a shock to the system, that's for sure.

That being said, there are twenty-four hours in a day, and understandably, you'll feel tired and constantly on the go for most of that time. However, I believe it's so important to schedule in some time each week solely for you and your parenting partner. One of the best things you can do when raising your child is to remain connected while doing so. Lack of time or busyness is not an excuse. To be totally honest, I'm surprised by how many relationships are splitting up these days (and by no means am I saying to stay in an abusive relationship; I would never suggest that); however, I'm sure many relationships could've been saved with a little more time, kindness, and attention, and by scheduling in and enjoying parent time together. Sure, it won't be like the early days, and you'll need to adapt to your growing family, but the more you make it a priority, the better it will be for your family bubble.

In the first year after giving birth, as I shared with you earlier, I was exhausted and recovering from my operation, but I still knew how important it was to make time to be with Nick. I wanted to stay connected (especially after the realisation from my social inventory), so I led the way and scheduled in regular time with him. Sometimes, we'd go for a walk; sometimes, we had a coffee and chat; sometimes, we watched a TV show together. We occasionally had a candlelight date night at home. Other times, it would be some mum and dad fun between the sheets (which I know can be a little taboo to talk about); however, staying intimately connected is often an important part of maintaining a healthy relationship. If we didn't schedule in this special time together during the early years and waited until I was in the mood, it would have rarely happened. I'd make a plan and let him know, and if the plan went out the window because the children didn't stay asleep, it didn't matter; the important part was that we were both making an effort to stay connected while raising young children.

Inspired Action: Schedule in time at least once each week to connect with your partner. You may even like to create a list together of the things you'd like to do over the coming year during your scheduled time. This way, you continue to prioritise the relationship, and during the challenging times, you'll more likely come together rather than push one another away.

There will always be events, birthdays, and meetings that you feel obliged to attend (and by all means go to as many as you like). However, if you try to please everyone by attending everything at the expense of time for you and your partner, please take a moment to think about what's best for your family bubble.

Perhaps ponder the following: In forty years, who do you want to be sitting on the couch with, watching a funny TV show? Who do you want to go on that overseas holiday with? How do you want your life to be? Who do you want by your side? If you think about these questions, you'll know exactly how to prioritise your time.

Remember that deep connection occurs by prioritising and creating little moments of presence over time. So, lovely mum, make time for you and your partner, and notice how the quality of connection shifts to a more intimate gear.

30

The Who Needs Me at My Best Right Now Tool

Let's be realistic: As mums, we spend most of our time doing things for others rather than doing things for ourselves. So I ask you, who needs you to be on your wellbeing A game the most right now? Yes, that's right: your children do. Forget pleasing everyone; narrow your focus to those who really need you right now. Everyone else can wait.

The main reason I began my journey into wellbeing coaching for mums was due to my time as a teacher and school wellbeing leader. In my teaching career, I saw the direct impact a mum's wellbeing has on a child's happiness and learning in the classroom. As a mum, I now know that logically this makes sense. However, I believe it's still totally underestimated in today's world and is rarely discussed in the education and learning industries. We all know to some extent that childhood anxiety, obesity, and disconnectedness are rising at a rapid rate, but as mums, we need to act now. Our children desperately need us to begin taking our wellbeing seriously. And no matter what you've been doing up until now, you can start fresh today; it's totally in your power.

Mid-2018, as I was writing this book, I totally fell off the wellbeing horse. A series of (what I perceived as unacceptable) events took me down. They consumed my focus, I wasn't at my best; I'd let my A game slip. I was deep in struggle and it took me a while to get back to feeling good again. I knew that I had to, not only for me but for my children, too. My family needed me to be at my best. I owed it to them, and I owed it to myself.

Inspired Action

Step 1. Decide that your children need you on your wellbeing A game right now.

Step 2. Forgive yourself for not prioritising this, and simply begin to do so.

Step 3. Take one tool from this wellbeing toolkit, and start implementing it today. Some of the tools are super simple; you can begin incorporating them right now.

Step 4. Have a wellbeing conversation with your family, sharing with them what you'll be doing. Let them know how you feel and why you want to do this (for you and for them).

The wellbeing approach will take some getting used to. Don't worry; if you fall off the wellbeing horse, you'll get back on again and again and again, until the wellbeing tools become ingrained in your daily habits. Will it be worth it? Without a doubt.

I totally know you can do this. The fact that you have read the book up to this point means you're fully committed, and you're about to take your wellbeing to the next level for you and your children. You won't look back.

Notes

Afterword

I feel so proud to be sharing this book with you. It's something I've dreamed of creating for a long time, and now it's here.

Regardless of what happens next, I'll feel successful simply because I did what I set out to do, which was write this book for you.

Now that it's complete, I feel like a new chapter is beginning. I'm excited (or as Madeleine says, "nervited," which is excitement with a side of nervousness) because I don't know what lies ahead. I suppose none of us really do, but that's what makes life so wonderful.

What I do know is that you have control over your daily choices. My hope is that after reading this book, you'll now feel empowered to live a more wellbeing-focused life. You may already be thinking about your wellbeing a little differently and starting to feel the shift that happens when you start living life on your terms. Remember, it sometimes gets rockier before it gets better, but it's so worth the ride.

If you've read this book, it's exactly where you're meant to be. There's something in here for you. Trust that what you've read is for a reason, even if you're not super clear on what it is right now. Sometimes, the message takes time to reveal itself. All you need to do is be ready to receive the message. Open your mind to this way of living. Know that true happiness is a possibility for you.

I believe in you; you simply need to believe in yourself. You're the creator of your life. Own it. Take positive action, and watch how your life transforms before your eyes. This is just the beginning.

I hope you enjoy achieving your wellbeing goals.

Rhiannon

Acknowledgements

Dragana, my old friend who I promised twenty years ago that I'd turn my life around. I kept my promise.

My friends, both new and old, for your beautiful support and belief in my work: Katie, Andrea, Kristy, Tanya, Rebecca, Jacqui, Sandra, Aimee, Jessica, Nina, Margaret, Danielle, Amanda, Mary, Jade, Julie, Johanna, Lisa V, Marie, Sam, Nicole, Veronica, Audra, Genevieve, Kylie, Claire, Narelle, Daniela, Lisa S, Vanessa, Lynne, Susan, Erin, and Gael. Thank you for being shining lights in my life.

My grandparents (all angels now), for your unconditional love and presence; it meant the world to me. I know you're still watching over me.

My parents, for believing in my work and cheering me on the whole way. Thank you for your love, support, and kindness on this journey. I love you so much.

My sisters, for being my best friends, for always making me laugh, and for your positivity and support as I brought this book to life. I feel blessed to call you my sisters.

My cousins and aunties, for being a beautiful village of support. I adore you all.

My in-laws (and Papa), for introducing me to spirituality and for raising such a beautiful son, the brilliant man I've been with for nineteen years.

My editors: Louise, for being with me right from the start of my book journey. I appreciate all your help, support, valuable input, and guidance. And to Liz for your support, kindness, and generosity in making this book a reality. I'll be forever grateful to you both.

My beautiful children, for helping me become a better person and for making my life a wild adventure. For being so supportive and believing that I (your mum) could actually become an author. I love you more than all the stars in the sky, and I feel so blessed that I get to experience this life with you.

My husband, for seeing the good in me when I couldn't see it in myself. For being by my side through the ups and downs, and for supporting me in following my dreams even when you didn't understand it all. I love you so much, and I'm excited about our next chapter.

Everyone I've ever known, whether we only met briefly or have known each other for a long time, thank you for teaching me so much in my thirty-nine years and for helping me to become the woman I am today.

Notes

Wellbeing Toolkit Extras

Wellbeing Reflection Activity

The Wellbeing Reflection Activity is the perfect check-in tool to help clarify where you are so that you can move forward and achieve your wellbeing goals with focus and confidence.

This activity is your opportunity to gain clarity in the dimensions in which you are thriving and in the dimensions that need a little more of your time, love, and attention.

The mums who've attended my workshops rave about this tool and often use it to check in on how they're doing throughout the year.

The Five Wellbeing Dimensions

Physical
Social
Mental
Spiritual
Emotional

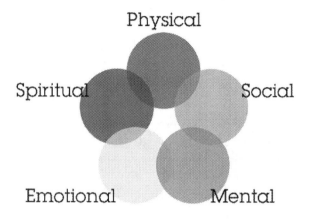

Take some time to write down your answers to each question in all five wellbeing dimensions.

The Physical Wellbeing Dimension Is All About Body

The Physical Wellbeing dimensions consist of exercise, sleep, habits, and diet.

When checking in on your physical wellbeing, ask yourself the following questions:

- How do you feel about the current state of your physical wellbeing?
- What are your strengths in this dimension?
- What do you see as your challenges?
- What's one aspect that you would like to shift/change/transform in this dimension?

Give yourself a rating in the Physical Wellbeing dimension out of 10.

The Social Wellbeing Dimension Is All About Relationships

The Social Wellbeing dimension consists of your family, friends, co-workers, personal/intimate partner, and community.

When checking in on your social wellbeing, ask yourself the following questions:

- How do you feel about the current state of your social wellbeing?
- What are your strengths in this dimension?
- What do you see as your challenges?
- What's one aspect that you would like to shift/change/transform in this dimension?

Give yourself a rating in the Social Wellbeing dimension out of 10.

The Mental Wellbeing Dimension Is All About Mind

The Mental Wellbeing dimension consists of thoughts, opinions, perceptions, and role-playing.

When checking in on your mental wellbeing, ask yourself the following questions:

- How do you feel about the current state of your mental wellbeing?
- What are your strengths in this dimension?
- What do you see as your challenges?
- What's one aspect that you would like to shift/ change/transform in this dimension?

Give yourself a rating in the Mental Wellbeing dimension out of 10.

The Spiritual Wellbeing Dimension Is All About Soul

The Spiritual Wellbeing dimension consists of true self and deeper connection.

When checking in on your spiritual wellbeing, ask yourself the following questions:

- How do you feel about the current state of your spiritual wellbeing?
- What are your strengths in this dimension?
- What do you see as your challenges?
- What's one aspect that you would like to shift/ change/transform in this dimension?

Give yourself a rating in the Spiritual Wellbeing dimension out of 10.

The Emotional Wellbeing Dimension Is All About Feelings

The Emotional Wellbeing dimension consists of love and fear.

When checking in on your emotional wellbeing, ask yourself the following questions:

- How do you feel about the current state of your emotional wellbeing?
- What are your strengths in this dimension?
- What do you see as your challenges?
- What's one aspect that you would like to shift/ change/transform in this dimension?

Give yourself a rating in the Emotional Wellbeing dimension out of 10.

The Five Steps to Forgiveness

Step 1. Willingness

Your willingness to forgive is the first and most important step of your forgiveness journey. By merely being here, gorgeous soul, you have decided to invest in your wellbeing. It's wonderful to be with you here and to be part of your journey to unconditional forgiveness, an essential part of everyday wellbeing. You're truly on your way to wholeheartedly forgiving yourself and others.

Step 2. Reflection

Before reading the forgiveness reflection below, close your eyes, place your hands on your heart, and take three slow, deep breaths. Before opening your eyes, say to yourself, "I am willing to learn to forgive myself and others. Forgiveness is a friend supporting me on my wellbeing journey. I open up to the possibility of experiencing feelings of ease, freedom, and peace. All is well."

When you practise everyday forgiveness, you're choosing to start fresh. You're free to forgive and start fresh, every minute of every day. The choice is always yours. Forgiveness frees you from the past and from all your negative choices. Today is a new day. You can choose to keep what (or who) is troubling you active today, or leave it like yesterday's news. Forgiveness helps release past hurts that continue to hurt you today. Forgiveness invites you to be more compassionate and accepting of your imperfect human self. Forgiveness is the highest form of self-love. It can dissipate grievances, resentments, annoyances, and all other forms of negativity. Forgiveness says I won't be defined by someone's past behaviour, nor will I allow my past behaviour to define me today. Forgiveness invites you to celebrate today rather than mourn or dwell on the past. The past is history. Today is now, and now is all that really matters. Forgiveness creates precious mental space so you can focus your energy on what matters most. It's a beautiful way to nurture your wellbeing. To forgive is to value your happiness and wellbeing. Forgiveness is the key to amazing wellbeing, and it's a moment-to-moment choice. My biggest hope for you is that you decide to embrace your forgiveness journey today.

Step 3. Forgiveness Inventory

You'll need a piece of paper and a pen for this wellbeing activity. On the left-hand side of the paper, make a list of all the people you would like to forgive, including yourself. Once you have completed your list, write on the right-hand side a reason why you want to (or feel the need to) forgive each of these people.

Step 4. Acknowledge and Release

Spend a minute looking over and observing the people on your forgiveness inventory. Place a heart around each of the names that you have on your list.

You may resist placing a heart around some names; if so, place a second heart around those names.

The two hearts highlight those who have hurt us the most. These souls are our greatest teachers. They need more of our love and compassion, more so than the others on the list. By healing our thoughts and feelings towards them, we heal ourselves and our relationships.

Step 5. Morning Blessings

Each morning, for the following seven days, spend a minute blessing those on your forgiveness inventory. Do this by sending each of them your loving thoughts and energy. Spend ten seconds wishing each of them well. Imagine they're surrounded by a peaceful white light. The morning blessing is a powerful activity because what you wish for another person, you wish for yourself; ultimately, we are all connected. This one simple forgiveness action has the potential to transform all of your relationships and therefore transform your life.

For Further Help and Support on Your Wellbeing Journey

- **Beyond Blue**
  https://www.beyondblue.org.au/
  (300) 224-636

- **The Butterfly Foundation**
  https://thebutterflyfoundation.org.au/
  (800) 334-673

- **Mind Australia**
  https://www.mindaustralia.org.au/
  (300) 286-463

- **Women's Health and Family Services**
  https://whfs.org.au/
  (800) 998-399

- **Health Direct**
  https://www.healthdirect.gov.au/
  (800) 022-222

Notes

Appendix

2018 National Read Aloud Survey Results
http://www.readaloud.org/highstakes.html

Notes

About the Author

Rhiannon Colarossi is an award winning and internationally certified coach and speaker who loves inspiring mums to nurture their everyday wellbeing. She founded The Wellbeing Web after her time as a teacher and School Wellbeing Leader. Rhiannon loves empowering mums to build their wellbeing toolkit and regularly runs workshops and events. Rhiannon lives in Melbourne, Australia with her husband, son Jonathan and daughter Madeleine.

To connect with Rhiannon visit her website www. wellbeingweb.com.au or say hello to her via Instagram @rhiannon_colarossi

Printed in the United States
By Bookmasters